Jordan
River
Partition

Jordan River Partition

71143

By
Georgiana G. Stevens

HD 1699
J6
,S 84

The Hoover Institution
on War, Revolution, and Peace
Stanford University, 1965

The Hoover Institution on War, Revolution, and Peace, founded at Stanford University in 1919 by Herbert Hoover, is a center for advanced study and research on public and international affairs in the twentieth century. The views expressed in its publications are entirely those of the authors and do not necessarily reflect the views of the Hoover Institution.

To the memory of H. C. S.

who first took me there.

PREFACE

Jordan River Partition by Georgiana G. Stevens, the sixth monograph to appear in the Hoover Institution Studies Series, is the first on the Middle East. The Hoover Institution warmly welcomes Mrs. Stevens into the company of the authors whose writings it has had the privilege of publishing. Long a resident and traveler in the Middle East, she has viewed its peoples and their problems with a sympathetic and understanding eye. If any problem in the region would defy even Alexander's sword, it is the implacable hostility existing between the Arab states and Israel. Part and parcel of this problem, as our author shows, is the question of how the waters of the Jordan River are to be divided among the riparian states, Israel and the Arab states of Jordan, Syria, and Lebanon. For years Mrs. Stevens has delved into the intricacies of this question. Her monograph, The Jordan River Valley, published in January 1956 by the Carnegie Endowment for International Peace, has been widely used and quoted as a standard work on the subject. But much has happened since January 1956, beginning with the Suez War later in that year; and the embarking of Israel and the Arab states within recent months on new enterprises for withdrawing water from the Jordan emphasizes the need for a resurvey. Mrs. Stevens has, I believe, met that need with the same lucidity and fairness that characterize her earlier works.

In the Hoover Institution Studies Series another monograph relating to the Middle East will appear shortly, an analysis by Professors Moshe M. Czudnowski and Jacob M. Landau of the Hebrew University in Jerusalem of the performance of the Communist Party of Israel in the elections for the Fifth Knesset in 1961. Studies are planned on the activities of the United Nations Relief and Works Agency for Palestine Refugees in the Near East (UNRWA) and on Algeria since independence.

vii

The Hoover Institution Studies are monographs designed to be building blocks for scholarship in various disciplines concerned with different parts of the world. These building blocks may be complete in themselves, or they may be treated as material to be incorporated later into a larger structure. With this in mind, the Hoover Institution is glad to receive comments, criticisms, and suggestions for change or improvement from interested scholars as the Studies come out.

George Rentz

Curator, Middle East Collection
The Hoover Institution

TABLE OF CONTENTS

I. PARTITION OF THE JORDAN RIVER

The de facto partitioning of the Jordan River, being effected as Israel and Jordan construct separate and somewhat parallel water diversions, once again exacerbates the issues posed by the division of Palestine itself. The conflict over access to water in 1965, like that over possession of the land in 1948, involves not merely competing nationalisms and ways of life but also the actual physical survival of two populations crowded into the cultivable stretches of the Jordan Valley.

Once more, as in the days of the British Mandate, the issue is that of the absorptive capacity of this poorly endowed region. On the Jordanian side of Palestine it has not been possible, even with extensive international help over sixteen years, to absorb the nearly half million Arab refugees who fled there in 1948. In Israel, a population of 2.3 million now lives where 1 million Israelis lived in 1948 after the Arab exodus from Palestine. But even with massive financial aid from the West and enormous expenditures of energy and ingenuity, Israel has not been able to achieve self-sufficiency in food. Part of the difficulty lies in Israel's effort to integrate large numbers of immigrants while maintaining a European standard of living; but her greatest trouble is scarcity of water.

ISRAEL'S NATIONAL WATER CONDUIT

Nineteen sixty-four was to have been the year in which the Negeb desert would begin to receive Jordan water, piped from Jisr Banat Ya'qub (Bridge of the Daughters of Jacob) in northern Israel through the 100-mile conduit completed the previous winter. But, although the long-heralded water flow has, in fact, started, it does not come from Jisr Banat Ya'qub, and very little of it will reach as far as the desert. Instead, the first stage of the flow, during which some 160-180 million cubic meters (mcm)[1] of water per year is being moved, is drawn from Lake Tiberias and will have to be used mainly to replenish the water tables along the coast. Because their calculated depletion was compounded by droughts, the tables are now so low that agriculture, particularly in Israel's vital citrus orchards, is threatened. Water rationing and strict government control of pumping in this heavily populated region have been in force for several years. Thus, the immediate need

4

to relieve the coastal water shortage has, at least temporarily, altered the emphasis on new settlement in the desert.

In addition to this overdraft on her underground water supplies, Israel has encountered two other natural obstacles to her water planning: (1) the salinity of Lake Tiberias and (2) leakage at the site of the first proposed reservoir at Bait Natufa in western Galilee.

Moreover, political obstacles forced Israel in 1953 to desist, at least temporarily, from using the fresher waters at Jisr Banat Ya'qub south of Lake Hulah as her takeoff site. This was due to the fact this site lies within the demilitarized zone between Israel and Syria, an area whose final sovereignty has not yet been determined by the United Nations. It was a Syrian complaint at the United Nations in 1953 that led to the suspension order by the U. N. Security Council. Subsequently, Israel moved her pumping site to man-hewn caves in a hill at Eshed Kinrot, on the northwest side of Lake Tiberias. This change has been costly, and its drawbacks are becoming increasingly apparent. Thus, Syria's objections in 1953 succeeded in both reducing Israel's sweet-water potential and adding greatly to the cost of her National Conduit.

Another difficulty arose after Israel drained the marshes in the Hulah region: the flow of the river there became so rapid, that diversion of its waters into the proposed conduit was technically impractical.

Israel's dependence on diversion of waters from Lake Tiberias has markedly altered the prospects for extensive development of the Negeb. Vertical economic expansion, which demands that every new water supply be applied to light industry, now has strong support from official proponents who engage in public debate with those officials who are dedicated to the horizontal extension of strategically placed farm settlements in the Negeb. The supporters of vertical development argue that, for every water unit received, light industry contributes to national production thirty times as much as agriculture. For instance, Aharon Wiener, Director of Tahal (Water Planning for Israel, Ltd.), in an interview in the summer of 1964, said:

> One farmer living on 13 dunums of land in the central zone of Israel uses some 16,000-18,000 cubic metres of water per annum. In upper Galilee this figure is 20,000. In the Negev, especially in hot areas where the soils are very permeable, the quantity may be twice as much.

These are very large figures, especially as the total
amounts of fresh water available to us are so rigidly
set by nature. Industry consumes very much less,
only a fraction of the amount that agriculture does,
although today industry is bringing in more than three
times as much of the national income. [2]

Mr. Wiener touches here on a subject loaded with political

as well as technical complications. Other scientists, notably

Professor H. H. Hayman of Tekhnion in Haifa, have pointed out

that technically the entire plan for diverting water from the north

to the southern Negeb is wasteful, because water losses from

evaporation in the southern Negeb are three to four times those

in the north. Professor Hayman has implied that the idea of mov-

ing water to the southern Negeb for agricultural purposes is based

on political decisions that ignore technical realities. [3]

Paradoxically, the former Minister of Agriculture, Moshe

Dayan, has bluntly stated the case for industrial emphasis. "Only

30 million cubic metres more of water a year will be available to

our agriculture five years hence. Most of the water to be pumped

from the Kinneret[4] is designed to replenish our underground

resources, depletion of which is threatened particularly in the

Coastal Plain afflicted by a steep drop in the water table in the

past few years."[5] Mr. Dayan estimated that food production would nevertheless increase, thanks to water-saving techniques

and more concentration on crops requiring relatively little water.

A few months later, the Director General of the Ministry of Agri-

culture, Mr. Ariel Amiad, corroborated Mr. Dayan's position.

In a statement to the Israeli press in September 1964, Mr. Amiad

announced that agriculture had been allocated 980 mcm of water

per year, and that this amount would not be increased during the

next five years. The stress would be on increased efficiency of

cultivation, and particular attention would be directed at expansion

of the citrus crop for export. Clearly, the greatest economy in

use of water would be required to increase these crops.[6]

THE PROBLEM OF SALINITY

The high salinity of Lake Tiberias (increased in drought

years) makes the water currently being lifted at Eshed Kinrot and

pumped south too salty for general agricultural use. This serious

situation has become a political issue in Israel. The question was

ventilated publicly in October 1963, at a symposium on the Water

Project sponsored by the newspaper Haaretz in Tel Aviv. The

tone of the meetings was reflected in the comment of one writer:

" . . . the salty waters of the aqueduct . . . have cast a pall on the joy of accomplishment. "[7]

At the symposium, the Project authorities listened to bitter comments on the salinity of the waters being moved at a cost of $110 million. Mr. Aharon Wiener explained that the salinity in Lake Tiberias depends on rains but ranges between 270 and 380 parts of chloride to 1 million parts of water. Some of the salt springs in the lake had been detected only during the preceding two years. Whereas about half of the chloride comes from visible springs near the edge of the lake, the other half comes from invisible seepage.

To solve the problem of salinity, several devices are being used: (1) mixing of fresh well water with that in the Conduit as it travels southward; (2) attempting to cap or divert the visible salt springs at the southern end of Lake Tiberias; and (3) boring under the lake and pumping the salt out. Such diversions will affect the fishing in the lake, but the need for water is so great that this disadvantage will not deter the water engineers.

Speaking at the 1963 symposium, Mr. Dayan assumed that Israel was using 90 per cent of her total water potential of 1,800

9

mcm. He stated that Israel's territorial settlement was already 90 per cent of the country's potential. Thus he could not envision the establishment of many villages between Beersheba and Bait Shean Valley to the north. He suggested the state was small, with a small potential. [8]

Whether this view is extreme remains an unresolved question in Israel. Meanwhile, some farmers and citrus growers have made a case for delaying use of the conduit water rather than risking further salination of the soil. They accept 170 parts of chloride to 1 million parts of water as usable, except for orange growing, [9] but object that even 170 particles per million (ppm) will eventually salinate the soil. Others have proposed waiting until Tiberias water can be mixed with converted sea water. [10] Some agronomists even suggest that desalted sea water, despite the prevailing cost of conversion, is worth using to save profitable crops. Thus Mr. Ra'anon Weitz, head of the Jewish Agency's Settlement Department, has compared the prevailing distilled water cost of IL 1.30 per cubic meter with the cost of Conduit water at IL 1.00 and found distilled water worth the price. [11] The estimated cost of diverting the salt springs in Tiberias is some

$6 million.[12] If this figure is added to the $110 million spent so far on the National Conduit, the figure for delivered Tiberias water will be even higher.

In spite of the cost and technical difficulties involved, many Israeli planners, rejecting Mr. Dayan's pessimistic views, continue to call officially for extensive Negeb settlement. The Negeb now has a population of 150,000.[13] The aim is to add some 10,000 farm families by 1970. Even so, the figure of 10,000 is much lower than that set before the National Conduit's actual potential became apparent. Thus, extensive development of the desert seemed much further off in 1964 than ten years previously, at the height of Israel's optimism about her absorptive capacity. In 1964 the official estimate of the total population increase for the next decade was 750,000. This figure is considered high by outside experts, who calculate that fewer than 250,000 immigrants will have gone to Israel by 1975, and that her total population will grow more slowly than is officially estimated in Jerusalem.

What these calculations indicate is that, in the next decade, there is not likely to be overwhelming pressure on the land in Israel. If this is so, Israel need not feel driven to any of the expansionist moves that her Arab neighbors fear. In light of this, the Egyptians' fear that dozens of strategically placed settlements might confront them in Sinai seems disproportionate for the time being. Neither the water nor the people will be available for such an internal expansion for "millions" of settlers envisaged by the Arabs. At most, 60,000 new settlers can be absorbed in the Negeb, provided 320 mcm of water per year can be delivered there by 1970.

Nevertheless, discounting a large population increase, Israel's water needs inevitably will grow as she strives for industrialization. It is a question, however, whether Israel any longer expects to rely on Jordan waters for her future industrial needs. The emphasis today is on scientific means of desalting sea water.

THE ARAB STAND

In view of the foregoing, why are the Arab states more united than ever in their opposition to Israel's water diversion works? At the time of writing, they threaten to frustrate Israel by damming up or attempting to divert the headwaters of the Jordan River system, most of which are in Arab countries. This is their alternative to war, agreed on in Cairo at the meeting of heads of

state in January 1964. Arab engineering plans for headwater

diversion, which have been in the making since 1951, are being

revised to alter the courses of the Hasbani in Lebanon and of the

Baniyas in Syria. Should this be accomplished, Israel would bene-

fit primarily from the flood waters these streams contribute to the

Jordan but would be deprived of a substantial portion of the normal

flow of these rivers.

Since nature and politics have already frustrated Israel's

original larger dreams of making the entire desert bloom and of

making it a strong local defense line, the present Arab reaction

appears puzzling to many outside the region. However, disputes

over river basin development elsewhere in the world should pro-

vide clues to the Arab position on the Jordan question. One such

clue is the customary assumption that lands in a given river basin

have prior claims to its waters. As one report on the Jordan has

put it:

> . . . the waters in a catchment area should not be
> diverted outside that area unless the requirements
> of all those who use or genuinely intend to use, the
> waters within the area have been satisfied. [14]

Thus the Arab argument against Israel's diversion of any water out of the Jordan Basin rests on the grounds that the lands in the basin itself need all the water available and that there is no potential surplus for Israel's Negeb desert.

ISRAEL AND A UNIFIED PLAN

The Israeli argument for her present water program rests on a quantitative water allocation proposed first in the United Nations, and later in a plan evolved in the course of negotiations sponsored by the United States government between 1953 and 1955. This was the Jordan Valley Unified Plan of 1955, often popularly named after its ambassador, Mr. Eric Johnston.[15]

In its final form, this Plan apportioned some 60 per cent of the water of the Jordan River system to the Arab riparian states and about 40 per cent to Israel. This division was, at one point, accepted by technicians on both sides. While there was no formal document to this effect, Mr. Johnston did receive the acquiescence of both sides in the formula allotting the following shares of the system's waters:

Jordan	480 mcm/year
Syria	132 mcm/year
Lebanon	35 mcm/year
Israel	The residue after these amounts claimed as necessary by the Arab riparians. This residual amount would vary with rains, evaporation, and droughts, but was estimated at some 466 mcm. This was a reduction from Israel's last-ditch claims to some 550 mcm from the system, but it represented a compromise over the Arab technicians' original proposal of a 20 per cent share for Israel.

The Johnston Plan was concerned with the over-all development to the fullest possible extent of the meager waters of the Jordan Basin, within the basin, for the benefit of all involved. These included the Syrians and Lebanese as riparians, but more particularly the Jordanians and the great number of unsettled Palestinian refugees in Jordan, as well as the Israelis. The plan did not include provisions for moving water out of the Jordan watershed--an Israeli idea strongly resisted by all the Arab countries. However, at one stage late in the negotiations, when Ambassador Johnston demonstrated that Israel could use her share of the waters inside the basin, the Arab technicians showed understanding and conceded, at that time, that Israel might do whatever she liked with her share, provided in-basin needs were fully satisfied.

DISTRIBUTION OF WATER UNDER VARIOUS PLANS TO DEVELOP JORDAN VALLEY

SOURCE OF WATERS OF JORDAN WATERSHED — 23% / 77%

DISTRIBUTION OF WATERS OF JORDAN WATERSHED TVA PLAN — 1953 — 33% / 67%

ARAB PLAN — 1954 — 20% / 80%

ISRAEL 7-YEAR PLAN 1953 — 50%

FINAL JORDAN VALLEY PLAN — OCT. 1955 — 40% / 60%

ISRAEL   ARAB STATES (Jordan, Lebanon, & Syria)

THE UNIFIED JORDAN VALLEY PLAN

The negotiations conducted by Ambassador Johnston between 1953 and 1955 have more than historic interest: 1. They marked the beginning of an important stage in American involvement in Middle Eastern affairs. 2. They set a general pattern for peaceful division of a vital natural resource through patient negotiation. 3. They demonstrated the great sensitivity of the water question in the Middle East. As Mr. Johnston undertook his first mission to the area, this political sensitivity over water became immediately apparent. This fact, in turn, had a sobering effect in Washington, where it had been hoped in the early years after the partition of Palestine that the two peoples involved could be brought to some economic accommodation with American financial help.

It was in 1953, under strong congressional pressure to liquidate the Palestinian refugee problem, that the Eisenhower administration enlisted Mr. Eric Johnston, chairman of the International Advisory Board of the Technical Cooperation Administration, to carry water development proposals to the Arab states and Israel. It was hoped that all concerned could be interested in a

17

regional water plan that would benefit the riparian Arab states on the Jordan, the Israelis, and the Palestinian refugees by opening up new lands for cultivation.

To accomplish this mission, Mr. Johnston was given ambassadorial rank as the President's representative and was armed with a freshly drawn plan for the Jordan system. Entitled The Unified Development of the Jordan Valley Region, it bore an introductory note signed by Leslie J. Carver, acting director of the United Nations Relief and Works Agency for Palestine (UNRWA), and a letter of transmittal signed by Gordon Clapp, chairman of the board of TVA, under whose direction the plan had been devised. The study reviewed the various plans for the Jordan Valley then in existence and attempted to reconcile them on a basis of practicality and economy.

Mr. Johnston's first trip in 1953 met with a cool reception in the area. It came at a time when feeling ran high on both sides over Israel's plans to channel water out of the Hulah region, and just after a serious Israeli raid that killed some fifty villagers in the Jordanian village of Qibyah. This was in the period of Israeli military retaliations against Jordanian infiltrators in border areas.

18

The time thus was most unpromising for calm and concerted water planning.

Mr. Johnston, in this first approach, was faced with the task of gaining a hearing among Arab officials who were in a state of alarmed anger over the Qibyah affair and of anxiety over Israel's channeling of a part of the Jordan River out of its course. It took the utmost persuasion, in the name of President Eisenhower, to secure a hearing for Mr. Johnston in Amman, Beirut, and Damascus. Only on being assured that they need not contemplate any direct dealings with Israel over water, were the Arab governments persuaded to listen to the Johnston proposals. From the beginning of the talks it was plain that any water scheme involving Arab acquiescence would have to be carried forward under neutral or United Nations authority. Any other course implying cooperation with Israel or breaking of the Arab boycott of that country was totally unacceptable. On his first trip, then, Mr. Johnston was able to open discussions on the only possible basis, namely, as a neutral spokesman, and to induce all concerned to study the Unified Plan and make counterproposals of their own.

In talking with the Israelis, Mr. Johnston had to try to persuade them to harness their own extensive water plans to some internationally approved division of the Jordan waters that would prevent violence over the Jordan. The political climate in Israel at that time is illustrated in a "Background Note" issued by the Embassy in Washington in October 1953, which stated that while Israel stood ready to negotiate an interstate agreement on water, "it cannot . . . be expected to freeze all its development in the hope that the other states may some day be prepared to hold such discussions. "

A broadcast statement by Foreign Minister Sharett on November 30, 1953, clarified the Israeli government's position further:

> As to the question of regional water planning, we were the first who declared our willingness to sit together with our three neighbors who may have joint water interests with us . . . for the purpose of discussing a regional arrangement based on a just distribution of water sources. As long as no arrangement of this sort exists because the neighbor states refuse to meet with Israel, we consider ourselves free to use the water of the rivers which flow in our country as our property. We are convinced that the undisturbed continuation of Israeli development works constitutes perhaps the most effective method to insure regional cooperation. In the same manner, however, as Israel does not give up its freedom of policy and independent opinion in exchange for American aid . . . it cannot be attracted by immediate foreign aid to such an extent that it would give up the prospects of its future development and consolidation.

Within Israel, Foreign Minister Sharett appeared to favor

serious consideration of the Johnston proposals on political grounds.

Two possible advantages to Israel were (1) improved relations with

her Arab neighbors that might result from joint use of Jordan

waters and (2) the international financing of water development Mr.

Johnston was able to offer. Mr. Sharett even hoped that an even-

tual accommodation over water might make it possible for Israel

to negotiate with Lebanon for an exchange of power for water from

the Litani River. Such an exchange had been basic in all Zionist

economic planning.

Counterproposals

To the extent that Mr. Johnston was able to stimulate coun-

terproposals to the Main Plan, his first efforts were successful.

In the case of the Arabs, he was aided by active cooperation from

the new Egyptian Revolutionary government. Stopping off in Cairo

on his way to the Near East, Mr. Johnston appealed to the leaders

of the military junta to use their influence toward a negotiated set-

tlement of the river issue. The Egyptians, anxious to assert their

role as leaders of the Arab bloc, moved to set up an Arab League

Technical Committee on water under the chairmanship of an

Egyptian engineer, Dr. Mohammed Selim, then Secretary General

of Egypt's National Production Council.

Arab Plans

In March 1954, the Arab Plan for Development of the Water

Resources in the Jordan Valley appeared. This document was the

first all-Arab regional water plan and was remarkable for the fact

that it recognized Israel's rights as a riparian state to a share of

Jordan waters--i. e. , the plan implicitly ignored the Arab boycott

and allocated a small share of waters to Israel.

At the same time, a commentary on the Johnston proposals

was issued by the Arab Palestine Office in Beirut. The commen-

tary stressed the fact that, since the Arab states already were

riparians with regard to the rivers of the Levant, it was unreason-

able to expect them to accept a plan that would deprive them of a

share in these waters. However, the more constructive proposals

in the Arab Plan devised in Cairo became the basic document from

which the Arab governments continued discussions with Ambassador

Johnston. Under the Arab Plan, the Hasbani River in Lebanon

would be used for power and irrigation; Israeli land in the Hulah

region would receive Jordan water; and two storage dams on the

Yarmuk would be used to generate power and irrigate Jordan Valley lands.

The Arab spokesmen agreed to the use of Lake Tiberias as a storage site for surplus waters, but their engineers rejected it as the main storage facility since it lies wholly within Israel. The plan called for irrigation canals from Tiberias to the lower Jordan Valley. Its principal difference from the Johnston Plan was that it awarded Israel only 20 per cent as against about 35 per cent of the waters to be developed.[16]

Israeli Plans

Israel's answer to the Johnston proposals was the Cotton Plan, named for the American engineer, J. S. Cotton, who was then a consultant to the Tel Aviv government. This plan called for use of one-third of the waters of the Litani. It included a diversion canal from Jisr Banat Ya'qub in the Hulah region as well as larger diversions from the Jordan headwaters to a reservoir at Sahl Battuf near Nazareth, plus the canals then under construction on the Israel coastal plain. Under the Cotton Plan, Lake Tiberias' known salinity would be reduced by the introduction of fresh water from the Litani River. The Jordan headwaters channelled into storage at Sahl Battuf would be picked up and moved eventually to the Negeb. Jordan's needs were to be met by drawing Yarmuk water through a canal system under Jordan's control.

The Cotton Plan would, in effect, draw on the headwaters of the Jordan system, that is, the Hasbani and the Baniyas, for fresh water; and it would reach north outside the Jordan Basin to the Litani in Lebanon for further sources of fresh water. In Israeli eyes, this ambitious plan was a natural sequel to the plans of the early Zionists, who had foreseen that the viability of a Jewish state in Palestine would depend on its ability to take northern waters from surrounding territories southward to Palestine.

Background to Israeli Plans. Far-sighted Zionist planners had begun as early as 1916 to urge the British government to claim all of the Jordan for Palestine. They also pressed to have the Litani River demarcate Palestine's northern frontier with Lebanon. At the time of the disposition of the Ottoman territories in the Near East in 1918, the King-Crane Commission, sent by President Wilson to study the question, reported the Zionist argument for a Jewish National Home in Palestine:

> . . . there is no need of displacing the present population, for with afforestation, modern methods of

agriculture, utilization of water-power, réclamation
of waste lands, scientific irrigation, and the like, the
land can contain several times its present number of
inhabitants. . . .[17]

Zionist hopes of a "Greater Palestine" were, however,

thwarted when--at French insistence--the frontiers of Lebanon and

Syria were set south of the Litani and west of the slopes of Mt.

Hermon, thereby leaving the headwaters of the Jordan system in

these French-mandated territories. Moreover, the Mandates, in

their final form, provided that the United Kingdom could set up a

separate state east of the Jordan River. In this state of Transjor-

dan, the United Kingdom could "postpone or withhold" application

of those clauses of the Mandate for Palestine that called for estab-

lishment of a "Jewish National Home."

In this fashion, the Mandate Powers had set the stage for a

future contest over water that time has greatly exacerbated. Jor-

dan at that time was a pastoral country where development of

water resources did not seem urgent. Within Palestine, however,

and at Zionist councils in London, the question of water for the

Promised Land was paramount. At stake was the actual absorptive

capacity of the country to which the Zionists looked for an eventual

established homeland. Yet the Jewish Agency for Palestine, set up in 1929 with the purpose of opening up new lands to Jewish settlers, was confronted by the Mandate government's fixed conception of the limits of possible settlement.

The Mandate government instituted a number of surveys to discover the actual water potential in Palestine, as a basis for settlement plans. Although nothing concrete came of these studies, they are of historical interest as a first positive indication of the Mandatory Power's effort to expand Palestine's absorptive capacity with a view to facilitating Jewish immigration in accordance with the promises of the Balfour Declaration and the Mandate for Palestine. One important result was the first hydrographic survey of the Jordan Valley. This work was conducted by M. G. Ionides, Director of Development in the government of Transjordan, from 1937 to 1939.

Briefly, Mr. Ionides found that the only way to provide a substantial increase of arable land in the Jordan Valley was irrigation of the area between Lake Tiberias and the Dead Sea. He proposed diversion of water from the Yarmuk, with a feeder canal from Lake Tiberias, which would be used as a reservoir. By this means, he estimated, 75,000 new acres on the East Bank of the

Jordan could be irrigated; a similar canal could water lands on the West Bank in Palestine.

Such modest possibilities of growth seemed hopelessly inadequate to Zionist planners. Events in Europe in the late thirties were then forcing more and more European Jews to seek refuge in Palestine. Hence the issue of water became a daily preoccupation in Zionist councils. By 1943 they had engaged the services of a number of water experts, of whom the best known was Walter Clay Lowdermilk of the Soil Conservation Service of the United States. In 1944, Dr. Lowdermilk published a small but important book entitled Palestine, Land of Promise, in which he endorsed the most optimistic Zionist contentions about Palestine's agricultural potential. He outlined a plan for canalization of the Upper Jordan and the Yarmuk and Zarqa rivers around both sides of the Jordan Valley. He also proposed that Mediterranean water be introduced into the rift valley of the Jordan for power production. He estimated that the resulting power would amount to some billion kilowatt hours per year. Finally, he suggested a regional approach to water planning by drawing on then unused Jordan headwaters in Lebanon, Syria, and Jordan.

Dr. Lowdermilk believed that by all these means the full development of the Jordan Valley and adjoining drainage areas could, in time, provide farms and industries to support 4 million Jewish refugees in addition to the 1. 8 million Arabs and Jews living in Palestine in the early forties. Thus, Dr. Lowdermilk offered technical support to the Zionists' dream of ingathering of the Diaspora and raised their hopes at a crucial moment in Near East history. In a variety of forms and with some modifications, Dr. Lowdermilk's theories about water use in Palestine have become official doctrine since Israel's establishment in 1948.

It is not surprising, therefore, that in response to Ambassador Johnston's approaches in 1953 the Israeli government should have offered yet another version of these plans that included use of waters from adjacent countries. On one point Mr. Johnston was, however, unable to agree with Israel's position: this was with regard to the Litani, which--he insisted--was a national river within the boundaries of Lebanon. The remaining very wide differences between the Arab Plan for the Jordan Valley and the Cotton Plan presented by Israel made the subsequent negotiations exceedingly difficult.

Outcome of the Johnston
Negotiations, 1955

Throughout the remainder of his mission, both in the Near East and in Washington, Ambassador Johnston's efforts were directed at finding some common ground acceptable to both sides. By June 1954, he had reached certain broad agreements with the Arab representatives on (1) the need for a master plan for the Jordan Valley; (2) the need to raise the living standards of the countries concerned and of the Arab refugees, without prejudicing the latter's rights; (3) allocation of water among the countries on the basis of its potential beneficial use within the Jordan Basin; (4) storage on the Yarmuk River as well as at Lake Tiberias; and (5) international control over water withdrawals.

Israel's position at that time was based on the principle that water should be allocated only where it could be used and not as a "political bribe." Claims of efficiency and utility dominate a government critique of the Johnston Plan entitled Technical Comments of the Government of Israel on the Jordan Valley Unified Development Plan. This paper, produced in June 1954, contended that the "Unified Plan" was not justified on technical grounds.

Israel also objected to any suggestion of United Nations supervision of water withdrawals. The prospect of an international authority or water master was most unpalatable to her. Yet Israel supported the idea of a regional approach, with the provision that it should guarantee her own water rights and facilitate permanent resettlement of the Arab refugees in Arab states.

Through the remainder of 1954 and until late fall 1955, Mr. Johnston's efforts continued. During this period they were somewhat simplified by a fresh engineering study undertaken by the Jordanian government with United States assistance. This was the Baker-Harza study, carried out by the Michael Baker, Jr. Company of Rochester, N.Y., and the Harza Company of Chicago, which comprised a complete soil and hydrology survey of Jordan. The Baker-Harza findings were helpful because they found more irrigable lands in the Jordanian areas of the valley than had previously been estimated. But at the same time, it was calculated that less water per acre would be required to put these lands into production than had been expected. This provided a scientific basis for estimating that some 125,000 potentially arable acres existed on the Jordanian side of the valley, and that they could be watered efficiently with the amount of water allocated under the Unified Plan.

In the later phases of the negotiations, the advantages to Jordan could be outlined specifically in the light of the Baker-Harza findings. In the final Unified Plan produced in 1955, it was arranged that there should be storage both in Lake Tiberias and at a dam to be built on the Yarmuk River, probably at Maqarin. Distribution was to be so contrived that neither side would have physical control over the share available to the other. The Arab states were promised that a water master would supervise pumping. The Israelis had to face the fact that their original ideas were to be compromised for the sake of order along the Jordan. At least the withdrawals from the system that were allocated to them would have the sanction of Washington.

In retrospect, Ambassador Johnston seems to have achieved a fairly wide area of compromise over water allocations by the time his mission ended in 1955. His dealings were fortified by the offer of United States funds to cover the two-thirds of the cost of the series of dams and canals in the final plan which, it was then estimated, would amount to a total of $200 million. Had he succeeded in obtaining final ratification of the plan, an efficient use of the Jordan River system would have been accomplished. In that case, the total cost would have been less than the present cost of dividing the river, which may finally be about double or $400 million.

In 1955, however, despite inducements such as financial help and protection by a neutral supervising authority, the Arab governments could not bring themselves to give formal acceptance to an arrangement that would also help Israel's development. On political grounds they asked for time for further consideration of the entire plan. This was in October 1955.

The political question the Arab governments had to ask themselves was whether they were strong enough to back up their own technicians and accept a plan that was tantamount to tacit acceptance of Israel's existence. The answers differed. Egypt, believing the plan to be an enlightened approach to the refugee problem, urged the other Arab governments to accept it. Syria, with a new and insecure government, feared further internal upheaval if she seemed in any degree "soft" on the Israeli question, and therefore refused to agree to the plan. Lebanon appears to have balked for economic as well as political reasons. It was feared in Beirut that any easing of the situation with regard to Israel would lead to use of the port of Haifa by Jordan (as had been contemplated in the original Partition Resolution calling for economic integration of the proposed Jewish and Arab states in Palestine). Thus Haifa might become a serious economic competitor of Beirut.

In Jordan the great need for water development was the overriding concern of King Husain's government; yet the regime was not sufficiently secure to take the lead in any accommodation with Israel.

Finally, the deep suspicion of American intentions in urging the plan and offering to finance a large share of it was exploited by the more xenophobic elements in the Arab states. The plan was depicted as a scheme to help Israel increase her immigration, and as a bribe to make the Arabs accept a strengthened Israel. In the end the Arab officials came to no agreement and simply referred the plan back to their technicians. Thus, the momentum achieved during the Johnston negotiations died out.

This was nine years ago. Today, in 1965, with Israel making successful use of her National Conduit, although still committed to the Johnston withdrawal formula, Arab objections run as follows:

1. The original Israeli plan to take water from the fresh upstream sources of the Jordan below Lake Hulah is believed to be still a part of Israel's water plan. Israel's long-range plans do call for tapping this source, and the size and number of pumping installations seem to confirm the Arabs' contention.

2. The present diversion from Lake Tiberias runs through lands which, under the Partition Resolution of 1947, were allotted to Palestinian Arabs. Since the Arabs, who then rejected the Partition Resolution now rest their case on its land allocations, they charge that Israel's use of a part of this land for the diversion line is illegal.

3. On further legal grounds, the Arabs cite the principles of equitable apportionment of benefits. To quote Dr. Omar Z. Ghobashy, a spokesman for the Arab side:

> The consensus of opinion among jurists is that the right of sovereignty does not confer on any state the right to divert an international river which passes in its territory to the detriment of the other riparians. [18]

Dr. Ghobashy quotes Oppenheim, a leading authority on such questions:

The flow of . . . international rivers is not within the arbitrary powers of one of the riparian states, for it is a rule of International Law that no state is allowed to alter the natural conditions of its own territory to the disadvantage of the natural conditions of the territory of a neighboring state. For this reason, a state is not only forbidden to stop or divert the flow of a river which runs from its own to a neighboring state, but likewise to make such use of the water of the river as either causes danger to the neighboring state or prevents it from making proper use of the flow of the river on its part. [19]

Dr. Ghobashy elaborates, saying:

It should be observed that it is not only forbidden that a state divert a river if this act causes substantial injury to another riparian, but it is also a recognized rule of international law that every riparian has specific rights in the waters of the river which flows in its territory. The riparian has vested rights, i.e., the right to the volume of water actually used by it for irrigation purposes, and it also has reserved rights to use some or all of the surplus quantity which is not currently used for irrigation purposes by any riparian state and which is lost by the river at its mouth. This also applies to surplus waters resulting from water developments which are saved by prevention of evaporation, drainage, canals, dams and better storage facilities. In this regard, Professor Smith, an English authority on the subject, wrote: "A riparian state is entitled to as much of the waters of an international river as she was actually using for irrigation prior to any claim by another riparian state."

This rule has been amplified in court decisions in the United States and become known as the right of "prior appropriation." [20]

The conclusion the Arab governments draw from this line of argument is that Israel's diversion of waters from Lake Tiberias "without the consent of the Arab riparian states and without consideration of Arab economic interests or prior vested rights in water appropriation, is contrary to international law, is a serious infringement of Arab legal rights and constitutes a threat to the peace and security of the Middle East."[21]

Since there are no universally accepted principles of international law governing division of river waters, it has been customary for riparian states to negotiate agreements among themselves. In the Middle East there have been a number of such agreements. One concluded in 1946 between Iraq and Turkey governs the Euphrates and Tigris rivers;[22] another reached between Jordan and Syria in 1953 provides for joint use of the Yarmuk, chief tributary of the Jordan;[23] and a third, the agreement reached in 1959 between Egypt and Sudan, provides for sharing of the Nile waters.[24]

The Yarmuk agreement of 1953 bears directly on the Jordan question, since it provides that Syria may divert water upstream to irrigate Syrian lands and shall share power generated by a proposed dam at Maqarin in Jordan. The agreement states that

"Jordan has the right to use within Jordanian boundaries water (from the Yarmuk) which is in excess of Syrian needs."[25] The agreement makes no specific reference to the plan proposed by the Arab states themselves in 1955 during the Johnston negotiations, under which some 17 mcm of Yarmuk waters would go to Israel for use south of Lake Tiberias.[26]

A major storage facility on the Upper Yarmuk, which was part of the final Johnston Unified Plan in 1955, remains to be built, if Jordan is to irrigate the lower stretches of the Jordan Valley adequately. At issue at the time of writing, as in the past, are both the height and the financing of the dam. Here again legal questions arise, since the Yarmuk forms the border between Israel and Jordan for six miles and Israel, therefore, has riparian rights on it.

4. Finally, the real Arab objection to Israel's water diversion is, of course, political. The one weapon available to the Arab states since their defeat in 1948 has been their political and economic boycott of Israel. Denying Israel the use of the main supply from Arab-controlled headwaters of the Jordan is an aspect of the boycott. If this denial could be accomplished, it would limit

37

Israel's long-term plan to carry northern water to the Negeb for
further colonization. The Arabs genuinely believe such colonization to be a threat to them.

Arab-Israeli Dispute over
the Jordan Sources

In 1951, the Arab states began to talk about organized
exploitation of the Hasbani River, which rises in Lebanon from
springs at the foot of Mt. Hermon, and the Baniyas, fed by other
sources there but originating in Syria. These two streams are
joined just inside Israel about seven miles above Lake Hulah by
the Dan, which has its source in Israel. Together these three
streams form the Jordan, which just below Lake Hulah makes a
sharp drop at Jisr Banat Ya'qub. On the way to Lake Tiberias,
the river falls almost 1,000 feet in nine miles.

Ever since the Armistice lines were drawn in 1949, numer-
ous military clashes in the Hulah region--between Israelis extend-
ing cultivation near the Syrian border and Syrians on the hills
overlooking the scene--have taken place over the use of water. In
the summer of 1951, after a skirmish in the Hulah swamps, Israeli
Foreign Minister Moshe Sharett stated Israeli purposes clearly:

"Our soldiers in the north are defending the Jordan water sources so that water may be brought to the farmers of the Negeb."[27]

Israel's whole program for moving water out of the Jordan Basin to the southern desert appears to the Arabs to cut across the plans of the Jordanians to make the Jordan Valley more fertile. In this aim Jordan has always had the unquestioned support of Syria and Lebanon. In 1951, Jordan first announced her plan to irrigate the East Ghor of the Jordan Valley by tapping the Yarmuk, the important tributary which runs between Syria and Jordan. Israel then closed the gates of an existing dam south of Lake Tiberias and started drainage of the Hulah swamps to the north.[28]

Two years later, Israel's attempts to alter the course of the Jordan by tapping it at Jisr Banat Ya'qub to divert it to a power plant at Capernaum set off the first serious round of water disputes in the U. N. Security Council. The projected canal would have run through the northern demilitarized zone between Israel and Syria. The Syrians, whose forces had been in control of the zone at the time of the 1949 Armistice, insisted in 1953 that under the terms of the Armistice it should remain under the authority of the United Nations Israel-Syrian Mixed Armistice Commission. They argued that Israel had no right to alter any feature that might affect exist-

ing Arab property rights or give either side any military advantage.

This insistence on the Syrian interpretation of the 1949 Armistice

Agreement somewhat obscured Syria's most serious objection,

which was related to Israel's diversion of any Jordan water out of

its natural basin.

In this dispute, Israel was enjoined by the Security Council

in the fall of 1953 to stop diversion from the zone, pending further

United Nations action. This action never came because of the sub-

sequent Soviet veto in 1954, but the debate foreshadowed continuing

dispute over the conflicting rights of the riparian states to the

waters of the Jordan.[29]

The Role of the United Nations

Even before the acute flare-up over the Jordan River at the

United Nations in 1953, the Palestine Conciliation Commission had

proposed in 1951 the creation of an international water authority to

supervise development and distribution of the Jordan River system.

Economic development in the entire region was obviously essential

to enable any significant number of Palestinian refugees to make a

living in the Arab states and to give Israel a chance to become a
viable entity.

The economic union of the two parts of Palestine called for
in the United Nations Partition Resolution of November 29, 1947,
had clearly become impossible after the bitter fighting between the
Arabs and Israelis in 1948. The Arab defeat during this struggle
and Israel's conquest of 2,000 square miles beyond the 5,600
square miles allotted to her under the Partition Resolution can-
celled all hope of peaceful coexistence between Israel and Transjordan. King 'Abd Allah's subsequent annexation of the remaining
parts of Palestine eliminated the possibility of a separate Palestine
Arab entity along the Jordan River that would be economically tied
to Israel.

With this definite separation of the West Bank inhabitants of
Palestine from the coast, occupied by Israel, attention was imme-
diately focused on the Jordan River as an economic resource.
This was particularly urgent, because about half a million Pales-
tinians had gravitated to the territory incorporated by King 'Abd
Allah into what was now called the Hashemite Kingdom of Jordan.
With no possible means of making a living, the refugees became

dependent on the United Nations Relief and Works Agency (UNRWA) for bare survival.

UNRWA's first move to relieve the situation of these Palestinians was undertaken in 1952, when it aided the Jordanian government in surveys for a dam on the Yarmuk River. The site for a dam had been discovered by chance by an American engineer, Mills E. Bunger, on a flight along the Jordanian-Syrian border. Mr. Bunger was attached to the U.S. Technical Cooperation Agency (TCA) at Amman, which was then attempting to shore up the economy of Jordan after the influx of the refugees. The anxiety of TCA in this respect and the concern of UNRWA to make some of the refugees self-supporting led to a pooling of efforts directed at river development. Thus TCA put up $929,000, UNRWA $856,000, and the Jordanian government some $200,000 (out of British loans) for the preliminary work on a dam for the Yarmuk at Maqarin, where Mr. Bunger had discovered a natural site at the junction of three small tributaries of the Yarmuk.

The proposed "Bunger Dam," as the project was immediately called, soon encountered political obstacles in the form of protests by Israel. Israeli spokesmen in the United Nations and in

Washington objected effectively that unilateral development of the

Yarmuk might deprive Israel, as a riparian state, of her share of

its waters, and that it might preclude cooperative development of

the whole Jordan River system. As a result, TCA and UNRWA

support of the project was suspended, to the bitter disappointment

of Jordan.

UNRWA's next approach to the economic aridity of Jordan

was more broadly based. The agency made a contract with TVA

for a review and analysis of all past proposals for the use of the

Jordan River system. The result was the "desk study" known as

the Main Plan, or the Unified Plan, launched as a set of proposals

under United Nations and United States auspices in 1953. The

underlying purpose of this plan was spelled out in the letter from

the acting director of UNRWA, Leslie J. Carver, which accom-

panied the document:

> Towards the end of last year it was already clear
> that the United Nations Relief and Works Agency for
> Palestine Refugees in the Near East would shortly be
> entering into a Programme Agreement with the Gov-
> ernment of the Hashemite Kingdom of the Jordan to
> reserve a very large sum of money for a scheme to
> use the waters of the Jordan and Yarmuk Rivers for
> irrigating the Jordan Valley and for establishing the
> refugees there.

Although the main outlines of the scheme had begun
to take shape, it was thought proper (in view of the
importance of the funds to be committed) to examine
all previous plans--of which there are many--for
utilizing the waters of the Jordan River and its tributaries, and to determine the extent to which the
projects which the Agency might be called upon to
finance were really economical and would not be
rendered nugatory by other projects undertaken by
other interests in the same watershed.

Mr. Carver's letter clearly reflected the desire to recon-

cile conflicting water needs in an over-all scheme. The entire

study produced by the TVA was designed to head off acute conflicts

over water and to offer alternatives to anarchy in the Jordan Basin.

Evaluation of the
Johnston Mission

Since UNRWA had no mandate to negotiate over water with

the riparian states and the Conciliation Commission for Palestine

(CCP) was immobilized for political reasons, it fell to the United

States to assume the responsibility for negotiating some form of

water agreement with Israel and the Arab states concerned. Con-

sequently, the Eisenhower administration offered its good offices

in presenting the Main Plan to the rival powers in the Middle East.

The story of Ambassador Johnston's missions has been

told in outline. In essence, his efforts were directed at orderly and economic distribution of the available water resources among Israel and her Arab neighbors. It was hoped that the dual objectives of the United Nations and of Washington (as the principal supporter of UNRWA), to assist the Arab refugees and help Israel get on her feet, could both be furthered by rational distribution of Jordan waters.

As can be seen from the record, the Johnston negotiations came close to success but finally foundered on political obstacles in the fall of 1955. One of these was Arab reluctance to give up the total boycott of Israel. Yet two water plans produced by an Arab Technical Committee, led by Egyptian engineers, had offered proposals that recognized Israel's riparian rights. [30]

At that time, Lebanon and Jordan--urged by Egypt--seemed on the point of accepting the final Johnston Plan, which had been revised to incorporate many features of the Arab Plan. They had accepted the idea of a neutral water master to supervise distribution, because they regarded such a service a necessary protection against excessive Israeli withdrawals. Ambassador Johnston believed he had the Arab states' acquiescence, if not formal agreement, in allocating approximately 40 per cent of residual waters from the Jordan development to Israel.

Even though political agreement never came, the Johnston formula for water sharing became a guideline along the Jordan after 1955. Some development works were essential to both Jordan and Israel and could be undertaken unilaterally by each without damaging the other or forcing the political issue. Israel publicly, and Jordan apparently on an interim basis, tacitly undertook to stay within the Johnston allocations in their water planning. Having received such assurances, the United States felt she could make assistance for water development available to both countries.

II. FIRST STEPS TOWARD RIVER PARTITION

THE EAST GHOR CANAL

Since 1958 Jordan has been building the East Ghor Canal,

which uses Yarmuk waters to irrigate eventually some 31,000

acres in the Jordan Valley. The total diversion is 43 miles long

and will take, by flow by gravity, 140 mcm a year. Through 1963,

the United States government had contributed $13 million in grants

to this project, and Jordan had put in some $4 million. An East

Ghor Canal Authority administers the project, distributes the

water, and regulates the size of farms receiving it by the yard-

stick of efficient cultivation and multiple farm ownership.[31] In

areas irrigated by the canal, three to four crops annually are

already being grown where previously only a single crop could

grow.

At the time of writing, Jordan has virtually reached the

limit of irrigation development in the Jordan Valley until a dam on

the Yarmuk can be built. The government has had a Jugoslav

firm, ENERGO, doing a feasibility study of this dam, and a num-

ber of international firms have tendered bids for the next more detailed study. However, on both technical and political grounds,

the dam's location and height are at issue. The United States,

which favors the dam, appears to base her support on some form

of understanding that Israel will receive a fair share of Yarmuk

waters. There is a technical guideline in cases such as that of the

Yarmuk, based on historic precedent of actual consumption use.

In the final Johnston Plan of 1955, it was estimated that, on this

basis, Israel had the right to 25 mcm of Yarmuk water for Israeli

farms in the Yarmuk Triangle.[32] Since the United States stands

on the Johnston allocations, she must inevitably stand by this fea-

ture of Yarmuk distribution.

Until recently, the most likely source of funds for a large

Yarmuk dam appeared to be the World Bank. But the Bank also

makes stipulations for assistance to international river projects.

It cannot undertake to finance a project to which all the riparian

states concerned do not agree. In the case of the Yarmuk, it

seems obvious that Israeli acquiescence will not be sought by Jor-

dan and that, therefore, an international agreement on the Yarmuk

dam will not be reached.

Several World Bank missions have visited the proposed

site of the Yarmuk dam and its auxiliary at 'Adasiyah. But Bank officials have not been able to evolve for the Jordan River system, as they managed to accomplish in the dispute between India and Pakistan over the more complicated Indus, an agreement that would formally regulate shares of water from the Yarmuk.

On economic grounds, the United States has favored a dam of about 300-mcm capacity on the Yarmuk. Jordan and Syria, however, have pressed to make it nearer 500 mcm. Meanwhile, after much negotiation, these two countries have reaffirmed their 1953 agreement on the respective benefits they will derive from the dam. Jordan has also received a Kuwait loan of $11 million to further the project.

MUKHAIBAH: THE FIRST YARMUK DAM

In the fall of 1964, discussion about a potential site for a Yarmuk dam shifted to a gorge at Mukhaibah, downstream from Maqarin. Here the natural contours of the river basin provide a suitable location for a low dam of some 200-mcm capacity and a power potential of 30,000 kilowatt hours (kw-h) per year. The projected dam would be some 1,150 meters long and, initially, 70 meters high; this could later be raised to a height of 90 meters.

While such a dam would not provide the amount of power

Syria had hoped to receive from the Yarmuk, the project does have

other advantages. It provides storage for winter flood waters of

the river. It is situated along a sufficiently low contour line to

eventually receive any waters channelled to it from the Baniyas in

Syria. However, its more immediate advantage is that it does not,

at this stage, conflict with any Israeli claims to the Jordan River

system, since water impounded at Mukhaibah would fall well within

the Johnston formula for Jordan.

Beyond these advantages, the Arab states are faced with the

political necessity of making a visible start on river development

to match the success of the Israeli Conduit from Lake Tiberias.

Such an early start is possible at Mukhaibah, because it is less

costly to build there than upstream at Maqarin. The estimated

cost of Mukhaibah is $28.7 million. All of this sum is in sight

from Arab sources, so that the project need not await international

financial aid.

For all of these reasons--financial and political--one may

expect that Mukhaibah will be the first all-Arab dam to appear

along the Jordan Waterway. Jordan thus will begin to consolidate her side of the partitioning of the river system without injuring

Israel. Flood waters of the Yarmuk will presumably continue to

flow into Israeli lands southeast of Lake Tiberias, as they have for

many years; but Jordan will have control of the flow.

In anticipation of the dam at Mukhaibah, Jordan has already

begun to expand the capacity of the East Ghor Canal so as to extend

irrigation in the Jordan Valley. This expansion, which will double

the canal's present capacity, is mainly a Jordanian project, employ-

ing local capital and engineering firms. This fact illustrates the

extent to which Jordan has progressed in economic development.

Further evidence of Jordan's progress toward building a viable

state is the government's extensive scheme for well-drilling and

experimental farming in an area stretching from Zarqa across

the desert to the Saudi Arabian frontier. With the help of United

Nations agencies, such as the Food and Agriculture Organization

(FAO) and the Special Fund, Jordan expects to carry out a full-

scale desert reclamation program whereby much of her population,

including the Bedouins, will be enabled to make a living.

Jordanian water development, except for the Yarmuk and

the East Ghor Canal, is under a Central Water Authority (CWA) that coordinates water planning and initiates such schemes as the well-drilling program. This authority was established to deal with the country's acute water shortage. Cities such as Jerusalem, Bethlehem, and Ramallah are actually paying as much as $3.50 per thousand gallons of water (in Ramallah) and even $14.00 per thousand gallons in Bethlehem in the summer season.[33] To relieve the great water shortage and reduce such exorbitant prices, the CWA contemplates desalting spring water available near the Dead Sea, if fresh water is not discovered by well-drilling. There are springs at 'Ain Fashkhah along the northeastern shore of the Dead Sea, 400 meters below sea level and 22 kilometers from Jerusalem, with a flow of 166,000 cubic meters per day, but they have a salt content of 3,000 ppm. Even so, it is estimated that this water could be desalted and piped to Jerusalem, where it would then cost $1.22 per thousand gallons. Before such an effort is made, however, more wells will be put down in areas above the Dead Sea in the hope that less salty waters will be found to provide for Jordan's West Bank cities.

THE ROLES OF NATURE AND SCIENCE

Both nature and science have contributed some unexpected and useful elements to a peaceful partition of the Jordan River system. The Israelis are finding it in their own interest not to draw more out of Lake Tiberias than the eventual 320 mcm agreed upon, because the water is so saline.

With respect to storage for the Jordan River system, Israel originally hoped that the main center would be Tiberias, since the lake is within Israeli-controlled territory under the armistice agreements. Eventually, Israel learned that she needed Tiberias for more than her anticipated storage purposes, as other sites in Galilee were found to leak. Israel has, therefore, modified her policy regarding storage on the Yarmuk, and one major point of potential conflict has thus been reduced.

One great difficulty at Tiberias is the lake's high rate of evaporation due to its size. Consequently, Israel is experimenting further with chemical means of arresting the rate of this evaporation. Spraying the lake with chemical film is one possible method, but nature has so far frustrated this effort, for Tiberias is windy much of the time and no surface coating can be sure of being effective.

Desalting

Science may come to the rescue of both the Arab countries and Israel, by ensuring economic supplies of desalted sea water within the next decade. So far processes such as electrodialysis, freezing and filtering, and reverse osmosis--that is, the squeezing of salt water through specially designed membranes--are still in experimental stages. But progress is in sight, particularly in the newer reverse osmosis process, which is relatively cheap compared with the others.

More spectacular desalting methods by means of atomic power are the subject of intensive studies in the United States and Israel. The cost of fresh water produced by means of atomic power depends on the size and location of the nuclear plant used. An advisory group to President Lyndon Johnson made public in April 1964 a proposal that extremely large nuclear plants be located at coastal sites to produce both fresh water and electricity economically. This group anticipated that by 1975 such plants should be able to produce several million gallons of fresh water per day at a cost of 25¢ per thousand gallons--a price that is not

economical for agriculture. But, such water at this price would

be suitable for domestic and industrial needs in large population

centers. Thus, size of plant and market for power and water are

important items in planning the use of desalted water. In Israel it

is currently estimated that an $80-million reactor would produce

fresh water at about 28¢ per thousand gallons. This is more than

the present cost of Conduit water from the Jordan, which is

between 16¢ and 20¢ per thousand gallons. [34]

THE ROLE OF THE UNITED STATES

Concern for a careful adjustment of needs and water rights

in the Jordan region has devolved upon the United States as the

chief financial supporter of both Jordan and Israel. United States

government aid to Jordan between 1946 and 1963 was $385 million.

United States government aid to Israel in the same period was

$957 million. The United States thus has been contributing sub-

stantially to the support of about 2 1/4 million people in Israel and

nearly 2 million in Jordan, adjoining states very poorly endowed by

nature. On economic grounds alone, it makes sense to encourage both countries to become more viable by means of water development. This interest and the desire to keep an inflammable political situation damped down have been the reasons for Washington's activity in the water dispute.

American funds for water works in Israel have been applied largely to general irrigation projects. In 1960, a $15-million loan to Israel from the United States government was granted for developing coastal water resources rather than for the pumping installation near Lake Tiberias. Much private American philanthropic money also has gone into Israel's water program. United States government money advanced for projects affecting the Jordan, however, has carried the stipulation that Israel observe the Johnston formula. Washington's political support for the National Conduit has been based on this same understanding.

To settle specific details of water management, Washington has sent American engineers to verify the feasibility of the Tiberias diversion and its compliance with the Johnston limitations. Thus, at the southern end of Lake Tiberias, waters could be released to flow into an existing reservoir west of 'Adasiyah, from which they could then be pumped by Jordan for use south of the lake. [35] In this way, Jordan could have access to her share of

Tiberias water, as arranged by Johnston, whether she formally

accepts the arrangement or not. Without this water, which would

have to come from a site above any point at which Israel would be

dumping salt from salt springs, many Jordanian farmers in the

area would be helpless, as they have already been deprived of some

fresh water by Jordan's own diversion from the Yarmuk into the

East Ghor Canal, which has made the stream bed below Tiberias

more saline. (Yarmuk water has leached salt from the lands in

the East Ghor.)

Joint United States-Israel
Desalting Program

A common concern for the improvement of desalting tech-

niques in the United States and in Israel has led to agreement in

Washington between President Johnson and Prime Minister Eshkol

to cooperate in future studies. A joint United States-Israel tech-

nical team has already been conducting surveys and defined the

scope of this program in Israel. Since completion of these sur-

veys, detailed engineering and economic studies are in progress.

In the words of the joint communique issued in June 1964 at the

time of Prime Minister Eshkol's visit to Washington:

It is hoped that, on the basis of these surveys and
studies, an economic desalting project of mutual technological interest, producing substantial quantities of
water for specialized agricultural and for industrial
use, will be undertaken by Israel with the active par-
ticipation of the United States. The International
Atomic Energy Agency will be invited to participate
in the programme from the beginning, including acting as an observer in the joint studies this summer.
As agreed by President Johnson and Prime Minister
Eshkol, the knowledge and experience gained from
this programme will be made available to all countries with water deficiencies.

In August 1964, it was announced in Tel Aviv that Israel

would base herself in the future "not on geography but on technol-

ogy," and would ultimately create "something like an artificial

River Jordan." This statement came from Mr. Shimon Peres,

Israeli Deputy Defense Minister, during the first round of meetings

of the Israeli-American desalting team in Israel.[36] A few days

later, the technologists themselves made an unofficial statement on

the order of magnitude of the proposed nuclear plant for distillation

of sea water in Israel. The plant was described as an installation

that would supply 150 to 200 megawatts (mw) of power and 80 to 165

million gallons of fresh water daily. The target date set for com-

mencement of the plant's operation was 1971.[37] Subsequent

announcements from Israel in the fall of 1964 gave figures within this range.

During the summer and fall of 1964, joint discussions were carried on, with General Zvi Tzur, former Israeli Chief of Staff, representing Israel, and Mr. Milton Chase, of the Office of Saline Water of the Department of the Interior, representing the United States. These two were joined by experts from the United Nations International Atomic Energy Agency (IAEA). As a result of these discussions the United States has agreed to participate with Israel in a study to determine the feasibility of constructing a desalting plant in Israel.

Desalting on a large scale must be considered in terms of years and millions of dollars. The immediate stage in Israel is the feasibility study now under way and expected to be completed in May 1965. Work on an actual plant is scheduled for 1967. No actual figures, but only an order of magnitude, can be established at this stage of experimentation. But the more optimistic esti-mates count on a scientific breakthrough that will reduce the pres-ent estimates of costs. These now are 35¢ to 50¢ per thousand gallons for water desalted by any process. Cost of water from

61

normal sources in Israel is about 20¢. Thus, desalted water would have to be reduced in price in order to be economic for agriculture. Any such water produced in the next decade seems sure to go to industry and human use.

In the present Israeli view, the program for atomic desalting promises an achievement to match Egypt's Aswan Dam. As commentators in Israel have pointed out, success in Israeli desalting will increase Lebensraum without impinging on neighboring territory. The hopeful technological step being taken in Israel thus relieves some of the pressure on the Jordan River system and opens up the prospect of a new phase in Middle East economic development.

Meanwhile, Israel's more immediately useful alternative plans involve desalting by conventional distillation methods but on a larger scale than is now being done. Costs of conventional means versus atomic power will presumably govern the ultimate choice of methods. Any funds given or loaned by the United States government, for example, would have to be spent on the most economical methods available; all aid funds in Washington carry such conditions.

Whether conventional or atomic power is eventually found to produce the most economical desalted water is still a question for the future. It is a matter of great concern to the United Nations, which has produced a study entitled Water Desalination in Developing Countries (July 1964). This study is the result of several years' investigation of reclamation of brackish water in desert countries, under the auspices of the Natural Resources and Transportation Division of the United Nations. Further indication of forthcoming concentration on worldwide water deficiencies is the designation of the years between 1965 and 1975 as the "Hydrological Decade" at the United Nations. For that decade it seems possible to predict that local disputes over sharing of river waters in arid lands will become technically obsolete.

In the present decade, however, it is essential to conserve every drop of water in countries such as Israel and Jordan. Hence, the unhappy struggle over the Jordan River system goes on.

ARAB PLANS FOR THE USE OF
JORDAN HEADWATERS

Of the Jordan northern headwaters, the Hasbani in Lebanon contributes 157 mcm a year and the Baniyas in Syria 157 mcm.

About 258 mcm come from the Dan, which rises in Israel and has a steady year-round flow from springs. By contrast, the base flows of the Hasbani and the Baniyas are only 20 per cent of the annual flow; the other 80 per cent comes from seasonal flash floods. Below Tiberias, the annual flow of the Yarmuk is 450 mcm. Under the final Johnston Plan, Israel was to receive 25 mcm a year from the Yarmuk through a canal into Israeli lands after completion of the proposed dam in Jordan.[38]

The damming and canalization of the Yarmuk do not present special problems, but any diversion of the northern Jordan headwaters is bound to be technically difficult and extremely expensive. The porosity of the rocky soil in southern Lebanon and northern Israel has already hampered dam building (on the Litani in Lebanon) and has limited the value of Bait Natufa as a reservoir in Israel. Any attempt to dam the Hasbani must take into account the permeability of fills or dams made from local rock. Canals in the region would require expensive lining, and without dams they would not be adequate to hold the flood waters that make the Hasbani unmanageable in the spring. Even though there are possible dam sites on the Hasbani, any barrier to the passage of flood waters would seem to be beyond practical consideration.

On the Baniyas there are no natural sites suitable for a big

dam. The problem is one of building canals deep enough to carry

seasonal flood waters away from Israel and toward the Yarmuk.

Again, cost estimates are almost prohibitive.

In negotiations on the river question with Ambassador John-

ston, Lebanon claimed it needed 35 mcm from the Hasbani for its

irrigation plans. Lebanon can easily take this amount before the

Hasbani enters Israel. Similarly, Syria then asked for 22 mcm

from the Baniyas for irrigation of farm lands in the Butaiha area

east of Lake Hulah. [39] This amount, likewise, can easily be with-

drawn by Syria before the Baniyas flows into Israel. The Arabs,

in their current estimates of upstream water needs, say they must

ensure themselves against future Israeli demands on the system.

As their own independent plans take active form, they assert that

any Arab upstream diversion will be a matter of legitimate self-

protection. Thus, the Arab League Technical Committee for the

River Jordan and Its Tributaries meets frequently to calculate

means and costs of ensuring their own prior appropriations, to

use the language of water law.

However, one difficulty the Arabs have in justifying their

headwater diversions is that the scheme is being put forward so late. While an Arab Technical Committee has existed for ten years, politics and other priorities of interest have until recently prevented its functioning. As a result, the hydrology and geology of the region around the headwaters have not always been understood, and plans have sometimes been made that may not be physically or economically feasible. This puts the Arabs at a great disadvantage, even if their legal claims to self-protection of Arab lands by headwater diversion are valid.

Money may no longer be the main difficulty for any Arab water scheme. Kuwait has already put some $15 million into the Arab fund for the Jordan. This fund, established by agreement at the Arab Summit Conference in Cairo in January 1964 (see p. 13), is to receive contributions on a proportional income formula. Thus Saudi Arabia and Egypt are high on the list of subscribers, while less wealthy states will contribute in proportion. The total estimates for any significant diversions, including a high dam on the Yarmuk, run from $190 million to over $200 million--roughly equal to what Israel would ultimately have to spend for her completed diversion to the Negeb.

Even with funds apparently available from Arab sources, the headwater diversion plan appears at this stage to be of problematical value to the Arabs. It must be assumed that flood

waters will not be wholly controllable by whatever works can be

constructed in Lebanon and Syria. The perhaps most outstanding

Arab expert on these matters, Dr. Mohammed Selim, chairman

of the Arab Technical Committee, has recently pointed out that

storage of an estimated 250 mcm at the headwaters would deprive

Israel of only about 35 per cent of her contemplated withdrawals

from the Upper Jordan.[40] Dr. Selim claimed that denying Israel

this amount would still leave her enough for an annual flow of

150-180 mcm in the Conduit, but would later prevent the with-

drawal of the contemplated 320 mcm. Hence, the ultimate effect

of Arab headwater diversions would be to halve Israel's supply for

her National Conduit.

On political grounds, the Arab Higher Committee for Pales-

tine has emerged from long silence to warn that headwater diver-

sion plans "will not practically prevent the enemy from seizing

sufficient water supply to irrigate the Negeb desert."[41]

More realistic Arab political leaders, under the stress of

renewed popular concern over the water question, now say it is too

late to go back to the Johnston formula. Many even deny they ever

considered it acceptable. At the same time, they are confronted with the de facto division of the Jordan and the Yarmuk rivers.

Their sponsorship of the appropriation of most of the Yarmuk by

Jordan and Syria has made these leaders a party to the partition

of the Jordan River system. In any preparatory moves to take the

river question again to the United Nations, for example, they are

well aware that the rules constraining Israel from use of the Jordan

River would also constrain the Arab states from making withdraw-

als from Jordan headwaters and the Yarmuk. The Arab argument

is that, whereas the Yarmuk diversion has an insignificant effect

on Israel, Israel's withdrawals from Tiberias and diversion south

of the lake seriously affect some 30,000 Jordanian farmers.

It seems significant that any order for execution of the

headwater plans must come from the Unified Military Command in

Cairo. This leaves the final say with the military representatives

of the Arab states, who are in the process of setting up this com-

mand. As became clear at the Cairo meetings in January 1964 and

the Alexandria meetings in September, neither Syria nor Lebanon

cares to initiate headwater diversions that would set off Israeli

attacks on them, unless they are guaranteed military protection.

Syria, particularly, resents her helplessness against Israeli strength. The Arabs believe official Israeli warnings that any tampering with the headwaters will be regarded as an act of aggression against Israel and bring retaliation. It is the task of the new unified Arab command to provide defensive forces for such an eventuality.

The military leaders involved appear, however, to be taking a practical view of their position vis-à-vis Israel. Here President 'Abd al-Nasir's realism has been decisive. There is general Arab agreement with his view that the water issue is part of the whole bundle of Palestine issues, and that it cannot be solved separately. There is also agreement that Israel has superior military potential, and that any military approach by the Arabs today would be doomed to failure. This was baldly stated by 'Abd al-Nasir at Port Said in December 1963:

> We will not be overbid. I am not ashamed to say that I cannot fight if I feel that I cannot really. If I cannot fight and then go out and fight I will only lead you to disaster. Shall I bring my country to disaster? Shall I gamble with my country? Impossible. I shall not bargain in this matter. . . .

On the whole Palestine question, 'Abd al-Nasir has repeatedly made it plain that he will not stake his regime on a hopeless conflict with Israel and those who support her.

With any immediate attack on Israel ruled out, the strategy has been to campaign diplomatically around the world to enlist support for the Arab position on the Jordan River. A number of high-level missions have visited world capitals to explain their stand and to seek wider understanding of the whole Palestine issue today. Thus, what looks to Israelis like a simple transfer of their legitimate share of Jordan water from one region of their country to another, is proving to be a political catalyst, reviving issues that today's generation of world leaders barely remember. However, since many countries of the world are plagued by water problems, the Arab diplomatic offensive may produce some results.

III. DELAYED CONFRONTATION

THE ARAB SUMMIT MEETINGS--
ALTERNATIVES TO WAR

The diplomatic offensive waged by Arab diplomats in world

capitals during 1964 represents a new phase in Arab-Israeli rela-

tions. This phase began with the Suez affair in 1956. One of the

damaging aftereffects of the invasion by Israel of the Sinai Penin-

sula was the hardening of Arab positions against further steps to

reduce tensions. The arrival and continued presence of the United

Nations Emergency Force (UNEF) along the frontier between Israel

and Gaza, and at Red Sea stations, have reduced the amount of

military skirmishing in the area. But the door has been closed

since 1956 to any meaningful approaches to the Arabs by third

parties seeking a way to peace in place of the long, uneasy armi-

stice.

Israel's withdrawal of water from Lake Tiberias, even in

limited amounts, has catalyzed emotional resistance to Israel even

further--it is another reminder of past defeats. In Arab eyes, it

seems to mean that the land bridge between Egypt and the rest of the Arab world to the east is irrevocably gone; that it will eventually be occupied by new Israeli settlements in spite of all difficulties. This feeling that Israeli water withdrawals in 1964 were as serious a matter as was the establishment of Israel in 1948, is so innate and pervasive that it demands attention from any would-be Arab leader.

Given the Egyptians' aspiration to lead the Arab political caravan, it was inevitable that Cairo should take the initiative in making the Arab response to the Israeli challenge.

President Gamal 'Abd al-Nasir had become responsible for the Arab response during the period of Egypt's union with Syria in the United Arab Republic from 1958 to 1961. In the spring of 1958, Nasir strongly supported the Syrians in their contention that Israel's work on a canal to take water out of the Hulah region through the central demilitarized zone violated the Armistice Agreement. The Arab case rested on the interpretation put on the Armistice Agreement by Dr. Ralph J. Bunche, former Palestine mediator, as early as 1951 when he stated that "neither party could validly claim to have a free hand in the demilitarized zone over civilian activity, while military activity was totally excluded."[42]

This interpretation has been sustained at the United Nations. Both without and within the demilitarized zones between Syria and Israel there continue to be clashes over water and land use. Even more serious clashes are inevitable in the northern demilitarized zone, if the Arabs begin to carry out their threatened diversions of the Jordan headwaters converging in this area. From the map in this book it is obvious that the Baniyas, for example, is so close to the northern demilitarized zone that any Syrian activity there is within easy Israeli reach. Similarly, any action by Lebanon to divert the Hasbani by building a dam could be challenged easily by Israel. The Israeli government has repeatedly warned that it would consider any major attempt to interfere with the flow of these Jordan headwaters as an act of aggression, to be stopped by force if necessary.

The problem of the Jordan headwaters thus confronts the Arab states with an inescapable dilemma. If they carry out their intentions and try to divert these streams away from their natural course, they risk what they regard as the certainty of Israeli attack. If they temporize too long, they believe Israel will be able to establish a prior appropriation right to the headwaters overflowing into her territory, thereby depriving Lebanon and Syria of legal recourse. In some fashion they believe they must soon assert their own prior rights to use of these streams within their own boundaries to the fullest possible extent.

The moment of truth for the upstream countries, Lebanon and Syria, arrived late in 1963, when it became clear that they had no choice; that they could not risk war with Israel over these streams. At that time, an appraisal of Arab military strength revealed its total incapacity to defend any river diversion works in the riparian Arab states. It was in the context of this harsh truth that Gamal 'Abd al-Nasir made his frank statement about not overbidding in a struggle where failure was bound to be certain.

The alternatives to war evolved at the First Arab Summit meeting called by 'Abd al-Nasir in January 1964. Meeting at Arab League headquarters in Cairo, the monarchs and heads of state of the Arab countries, including those of North Africa, agreed to finance future headwater projects in Lebanon and Syria and to help Jordan build a dam on the Yarmuk. As a protective measure, they agreed on a unified military command under Egypt's General 'Ali 'Ali 'Amir, to be financed by the members of the League. Finally, they agreed on establishment of a Palestinian political entity to

carry the banner of Arab Palestine, and on creation of a Palestinian army to come under the unified Arab command.

From the time of the First Arab Summit it was clear that
the symbolic threat posed by Israel's withdrawals from Jordan
waters had provided the strong political stimulus needed to revive
the idea of Arab unity. Once more Israel had forced the Arabs
together--in spite of divisions over Yemen, over Arab socialism,
and over who should lead the flock. King Husain and 'Abd al-Nasir
made up their long-standing quarrel. Saudi Arabia sent King Sa'ud
as a symbol of Arab brotherhood. Ba'thist Syrian leaders broke
bread with scornful Egyptian generals. In addition, the long-smol-
dering cause of the Palestinians who left home in 1948 received a
fresh infusion of support.

The Second Arab Summit, held in Alexandria in September
1964, underlined the spirit of unity and the revival of deep feeling
against Israel and her supporters. Syria and Algeria this time
pleaded for an "Algerian solution," to "liberate" Palestine immediately by violent action. Fortunately, wiser counsels prevailed.
On the constructive side, there was agreement on a joint Arab
council for peaceful atomic research, and on an Arab court of
justice. On the headwater issue, Lebanon won a year's grace to

prepare for any diversion works she might undertake. Jordan,
however, got full support for an immediate start on the dam at
Mukhaibah on the Yarmuk. This is to be the first and least con-
troversial all-Arab river project.

It is significant that the earlier decision not to go to war
over the Jordan River was reaffirmed at the Second Arab Summit.
The aim was to build a defensive military system. However, when
Egyptian generals suggested that Egyptian forces might be sent to
Lebanon, Syria, and Jordan to reinforce their defenses, there was
immediate resistance. The internal repercussions that might
follow the arrival of Egyptian soldiers needed no elaboration.
General 'Ali 'Ali 'Amir's idea of equipping all Arab armies with
Russian arms also failed to win acceptance in Jordan and Lebanon,
both of which still rely on Western arms.

What can be foreseen from all this is an escalation of the
Middle Eastern arms race, as Israel cannot be expected to refrain
from attacking whenever future Arab water projects seem to
impinge on her security. The Arab strategy is a cautious approach
to water schemes and postponement of a showdown while building
military strength. With thirteen Arab states now involved in these

decisions and committed to support any future action with money

and troops, this cautious policy seems likely to continue.

One further and more hopeful sign of the times is the inter-

est shown by Egypt in desalting sea water. The Cairo government

announced in July 1964 that meetings were in progress to plan an

installation to be built near Alexandria. Participants were the

head of the Egyptian Atomic Energy Organization and the Higher

Committee for the Desalination of Sea Water. In September 1964,

at the Third United Nations Conference on Peaceful Uses of Atomic

Energy in Geneva, the United Arab Republic announced plans to

build an atomic-powered desalting plant with an annual capacity

of 150,000 mw to produce 20,000 cubic meters of fresh water per

day. This illustrates Egypt's great concern to use any scientific

means available to produce water. These moves by the govern-

ment, announced while the Second Arab Summit meeting was being

held at Alexandria, indicate a realistic interest in water develop-

ment as such, apart from the emotion-laden question of Arab

rivers.

Israel's reaction to the Arab summit decisions has been

moderate. The government continues to stress the deterrent value

of Israel's military superiority over the Arabs. Beyond this,

Israel, while keeping a watchful eye on the northern headwater region, seems preoccupied with desalting and with the creation of "a second Jordan River" within the country. So far Israel has shown no disposition to take some of the sting out of her water withdrawals by making any moves to compromise on other issues, such as that of the Arab refugees. Such a move might, of course, fail to win a positive Arab response. But it has been seriously proposed, notably by The Guardian, [43] a paper friendly to Israel, as a suitable means of demonstrating Israel's interest in peace along the Jordan.

THE POST-JOHNSTON ERA

The post-Johnston stage of quiet, unilateral water diversion on the Jordan has come to a close. The Israeli pumping operations begun at Lake Tiberias in the summer of 1964 have set in motion another round of disputes that could lead, at worst, to war, or, at best, to submission of complaints to the United Nations. Since neither side wants war, resort to the United Nations seems likely.

Should the issue come to debate again, many of the lines taken by both sides will be familiar. Israel will point to her record of compliance with the Johnston Unified Plan; to her sovereign right to use her share of Jordan waters where it will do her the most good; to her willingness to negotiate with the Arabs who refuse to negotiate with, or recognize, her; and to her acceptance of Jordan's diversion of most of the Yarmuk River for that country's own use in the Jordan Valley. Israel insists that her own diversion from Lake Tiberias does not damage Jordan or deprive that country of any usable water. Israelis argue, therefore, that in the absence of a general agreement, which they seek, no state has a right to veto Israel's progress by denying her water to which she is entitled. Some Israeli leaders, notably Moshe Dayan, oppose the idea of a neutral water master on the grounds that: "This would only put a barrier between Israel and the Arab states and delay them from ever reaching a face to face agreement."[44]

There are in Israel in 1965, as in 1956, those who favor using her military superiority in another "preventive" round with the Arabs. Fortunately, Premier Levi Eshkol takes a firm but peaceful line. In his statement to the Knesset of January 20, 1964, on the Arab summit meetings, he said:

We have undertaken to remain within the framework
of the quantities specified in the unified plan--and we
shall honor this undertaking. According to principles
of international law governing water questions, the
refusal of one party to reach agreement with a second
party does not give the party that refused the right to
prevent its neighbor drawing its reasonable share
from a river flowing through the territories of a number of states. The accepted law pertaining to the
allocation of water does not recognize the right of
veto or the right to compel the second party to allow
its water to run to waste.

Basically, the Israelis stand on the proposition that they

have a sovereign right to bring in as many immigrants as they

choose and to use their resources, including water, to provide for

the third and fourth million. Thus, the real argument still is over

absorptive capacity and Israel's policy of unlimited immigration.

The Arab case against Israel's policy rests fundamentally

on the rights of the Palestinians who fled in 1948 and thereby lost

their properties in what became Israel. The frequently repeated

United Nations Resolution that calls for the Palestinians' right to

choose between repatriation and compensation has sustained this

Arab position.[45] Israel's refusal to consider Conciliation Commis-

sion proposals for carrying out this resolution has blocked any

approach to easing of relations with the Arab states. Thus, the

most recent proposals worked out by the Conciliation Commission for Palestine involved giving heads of refugee families an oppor-

tunity to state their actual preference as to repatriation to Israel

or resettlement with compensation elsewhere. At the same time

Israel was to have final say over admission of any refugees opting

to return to their former homes, so as to assure her right to deny

the return of suspected security risks. These approaches, devised

in 1962 by a special representative of the Commission, Mr. Joseph

E. Johnson, president of the Carnegie Endowment for International

Peace, met with outright refusal by the Israeli government.[46]

If the water question once again comes before the General

Assembly, the familiar debates over the Arab refugee problem are

also bound to be revived. It will be difficult for Israel to separate

the water question from the bundle of Palestine problems the Arabs

are prepared to lay before the United Nations with heightened fervor

because of the water issue.

In effect, however, the years of temporizing over the water

issue have not been wasted. They have provided a clearer under-

standing of the actual, as opposed to the theoretical, potential of

the Jordan waters. Ambassador Eric Johnston's efforts stimulated

the Arabs to submit, for the first time, a plan for water-sharing.

He proposed the idea of a neutral water master--an organizational concept that may become a necessity in the final stages of partition of the Jordan River, and one which any future United Nations debate on the matter is sure to revive. He also helped Israel to see that her expansive dreams of a paradise in the desert might be fanciful. Above all, Mr. Johnston introduced a means whereby each side in the dispute has, in fact, proceeded unilaterally quite far down the road to full water development, without detriment to the true interests of the other.

Finally, in the nine years since Ambassador Johnston left the scene, there have been technical developments opening up prospects for new water sources in the region.

Thus, the de facto partitioning of the Jordan River system can be looked upon as a holding operation that has prevented a "war over water" and given the Middle East time until technology can rescue it. This remains the best hope in 1965. Looking ahead, it is possible to see this pre-atomic period of water development giving way to a time of potential abundance for the parched Middle East. When that day comes, possibly within this decade, the struggle along the Jordan need not remain one of survival.

NOTES

1. One mcm = 810.7 acre-ft of water, enough to cover these acres to a depth of 1 ft with water.

2. Jerusalem Post Weekly, July 17, 1964.

3. Interview in Haaretz (Tel Aviv), Nov. 14, 1963.

4. Israelis frequently refer to Lake Tiberias as Kinneret.

5. Jerusalem Post Weekly, April 17, 1964.

6. Jerusalem Post Weekly, Sept. 18, 1964.

7. Haaretz, Dec. 6, 1963.

8. Haaretz, Nov. 1, 1963.

9. The sweetness of Jaffa oranges depends directly on the sweetness of water used for irrigation.

10. Jewish Observer and Middle East Review, Oct. 4, 1963.

11. Ibid. I£ = 33 1/3¢.

12. New York Herald Tribune, July 3, 1963 (article by Science Editor Earl Ubell from Tel Aviv). See also Jewish Chronicle, Oct. 25, 1963.

13. New York Times, Jan. 13, 1964.

14. Report on the Proposed Extension of Irrigation in the Jordan Valley, prepared by Sir Murdock MacDonald and Partners, London, March 1951.

15. The Unified Development of the Water Resources of the Jordan Valley Region, prepared at the request of the United Nations

under the direction of the Tennessee Valley Authority (TVA) by Charles T. Main, Inc., Boston, 1953. This plan formed the basis of the 1955 Johnston Plan.

16. Georgiana G. Stevens, The Jordan River Valley, International Conciliation, No. 506 (New York, January 1956).

17. "The Paris Peace Conference," Foreign Relations of the United States, XII (1919), 851.

18. Omar Z. Ghobashy, The Development of the Jordan River (New York, Arab Information Center, 1961), pp. 39-40.

19. Ibid., p. 40.

20. Ibid.

21. Ibid., p. 42.

22. U.N. Treaty Series, XXXVII (1949).

23. Yarmuk Treaty, 1953.

24. Agreement dated Nov. 8, 1959.

25. Yarmuk Treaty, Art. 8(B).

26. UNRWA Bulletin of Economic Development (Beirut), No. 14 (July 1956), p. 104.

27. Christian Science Monitor, July 25, 1951.

28. Ibid.

29. Security Council Official Records, Nov. 18, 1953, pp. 11-30.

30. The Arab League's The Arab Plan for Development of the Water Resources in the Jordan Valley (Cairo, March 1954), pp. 8 and 9, allotted Israel 96 mcm north of Lake Tiberias and 84 mcm south of Tiberias. A revised Arab plan of October 1955 included the same amounts.

31. J. L. Dees, "Jordan's East Ghor Canal Project,"
Middle East Journal, XIII, No. 4 (Autumn 1959).

32. New York Times, Oct. 23, 1955; Christian Science
Monitor, Nov. 2, 1955.

33. United Nations, Water Desalination in Developing
Countries (New York, 1964), p. 173.

34. Jewish Observer and Middle East Review, June 12,
1964; New York Times, Feb. 8, 1964.

35. The final Johnston Plan of 1955 allocated 100 mcm to
Jordan downstream from Tiberias. New York Times, Oct. 23,
1955; Christian Science Monitor, Nov. 2, 1955. See also Jerusalem Post Weekly, Jan. 17, 1964, and London Times, Jan. 22,
1964.

36. Jewish Chronicle, Aug. 7, 1964.

37. New York Times, Aug. 13, 1964.

38. New York Times, Oct. 23, 1955; Christian Science
Monitor, Nov. 2, 1955.

39. Christian Science Monitor, Aug. 20, 1956.

40. Lecture by Dr. Selim, chairman of the Arab Technical
Committee for the Jordan River, delivered at the Egyptian Engineering Society, Cairo, Jan. 2, 1964.

41. Mideast Mirror, Jan. 25, 1964.

42. Christian Science Monitor, April 2, 1958.

43. The Guardian, Jan. 8, 1964.

44. Jerusalem Post Weekly, March 20, 1964.

45. United Nations General Assembly Resolution 194(III),
para. 11.

46. See Joseph E. Johnson, "Arab vs. Israeli: A Persistent Challenge to Americans," paper read before the 24th American Assembly, Arden House, New York, Oct. 24, 1963.

SELECTED BIBLIOGRAPHY

Governmental Publications

Arab League. The Arab Plan for Development of the Water
Resources in the Jordan Valley. Cairo, March 1964.
13 pp.

Israel, Ministry of Finance. Data and Plans Submitted to the
Jerusalem Conference. Jerusalem, October 1953. 227 pp.

United Nations. Water Desalination in Developing Countries.
New York, 1964. 325 pp.

Books and Pamphlets

American Jewish Committee. Water and Politics in the Middle
East. New York, December 1964. 15 pp.

Burns, E. L. M. Between Arab and Israeli. New York, I.
Obolensky, 1963. 336 pp.

Campbell, John C. Defense of the Middle East. New York,
Frederick A. Praeger, 1960. 400 pp.

Dearden, Ann. Jordan. London, Robert Hale Ltd., 1958. 224 pp.

Goichon, A. M. L'Eau: problème vital de la région du Jourdain.
Brussels, Centre pour l'Etude des Problèmes du Monde
Musulman Contemporain, 1964. 127 pp.

Hurewitz, J. C. Diplomacy in the Near and Middle East, Vol. II.
Princeton, N. J., D. Van Nostrand, 1956. 427 pp.

Lowdermilk, Walter Clay. Palestine, Land of Promise. London, Victor Gollancz, 1946. 167 pp.

Peretz, Don. Israel and the Palestine Arabs. Washington, The Middle East Institute, 1958. 264 pp.

Rizk, Edward A. The Jordan Waters. London, Arab Information Centre, 1964. 24 pp.

Safran, Nadav. The United States and Israel. Cambridge, Mass., Harvard University Press, 1963. 341 pp.

Stevens, Georgiana G. The Jordan River Valley. International Conciliation, No. 506. New York, Carnegie Endowment for International Peace, January 1956. 59 pp.

Articles

Dees, J. L. "Jordan's East Ghor Canal Project," Middle East Journal, XIII, No. 4 (Autumn 1959).

Hirsch, Abraham M. "From the Indus to the Jordan: Characteristics of Middle East River Disputes," Political Science Quarterly, LXXI (June 1956).

Ionides, M. G. "The Disputed Waters of the Jordan," Middle East Journal, VII, No. 2 (Spring 1953).

Khouri, Fred J. "Friction and Conflict on the Israeli-Syrian Frontier," Middle East Journal, XVII, Nos. 1 and 2 (Winter-Spring 1963).

Peretz, Don. "Development of the Jordan Valley Waters," Middle East Journal, IX, No. 4 (Autumn 1955).

Schmidt, Dana Adams. "Prospects for a Solution of the Jordan Valley Dispute," Middle Eastern Affairs, VI, No. 1 (January 1955).

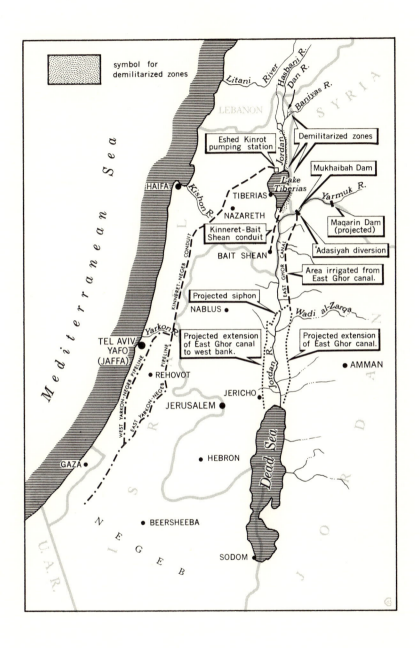

symbol for
demilitarized zones

Litani River

Hasbani R.

Dan R.

LEBANON

Baniyas R.

S Y R I A

Eshed Kinrot
pumping station

Demilitarized zones

Jordan

Mukhaibah Dam

*Lake
Tiberias*

HAIFA

Kishon R.

TIBERIAS

Yarmuk R.

NAZARETH

Maqarin Dam
(projected)

Kinneret-Bait
Shean conduit

'Adasiyah diversion

BAIT SHEAN

Area irrigated from
East Ghor canal.

Projected siphon

Wadi al-Zarqa

NABLUS

M e d i t e r r a n e a n   S e a

Yarkon R.

Projected extension
of East Ghor canal
to west bank.

Projected extension
of East Ghor canal.

TEL AVIV
YAFO
(JAFFA)

AMMAN

REHOVOT

JERICHO

JERUSALEM

Jordan R.

GAZA

HEBRON

Dead Sea

BEERSHEEBA

N E G E B

J O R D A N

U.A.R.

SODOM

KINNERET-NEGEB CONDUIT

WEST YARKON-NEGEB PIPELINE

EAST YARKON-NEGEB PIPELINE

EAST GHOR CANAL